North Carolina's Government

Printed in Mexico

ISBN-13: 978-0-15-366951-4
ISBN-10: 0-15-366951-9

3 4 5 6 7 8 9 10   805   13 12 11 10 09 08

SCHOOL PUBLISHERS

Visit *The Learning Site!* www.harcourtschool.com

Our National Government

READ TO FIND OUT **How are the branches of government different?**

The national, or **federal**, government deals with the whole United States. It has three parts, called branches. Congress, the **legislative branch**, makes the laws. The **executive branch**, led by the President, carries out the laws. The President also deals with other countries. The **judicial branch** includes all the federal courts. The Supreme Court is the most important.

The national government meets in the Capitol building in Washington, D.C.

The legislative branch makes the laws.

Every city and every state has its own special needs. But some things affect the whole country. These are the jobs of the national government.

The national government makes sure that we have a strong military. It prints our money and delivers our mail. It takes care of our natural resources. It sets up programs that help many people, like older people and those who have lost their jobs.

READING CHECK ŏ **COMPARE AND CONTRAST** **How are the branches of government different?**

State Government

READ TO FIND OUT **How does North Carolina's state government work?**

North Carolina's state government also has three branches. The legislative branch, which makes the state's laws, is called the General Assembly. The executive branch is led by the governor. The state supreme court leads the judicial branch. It makes sure that the state's other courts have been fair.

The North Carolina government is similar to the national government.

Legislative Branch

Executive Branch

Judicial Branch

The state government gives us services that we use every day. It builds roads and parks. It provides money for schools and hospitals. It sets up programs to help many people.

All of this costs money, which comes from the taxes people pay. One of the governor's jobs every year is to make a **budget**. This is the plan for how the government will spend tax money to provide services. The legislative branch has to agree to the budget.

READING CHECK **MAIN IDEA AND DETAILS** **How does North Carolina's state government work?**

The government makes laws to protect people. Wearing a bike helmet is a law.

Local Government

READ TO FIND OUT **How does local government work?**

North Carolina has many counties, cities, and towns. They are different in many ways. Some are small. Some are large. Some have many more people than others. Each has different resources and businesses.

Governments are chosen by the voters in each county, city, and town to meet their needs. For example, each county government fixes the roads in that county.

Local governments provide important services, such as police protection.

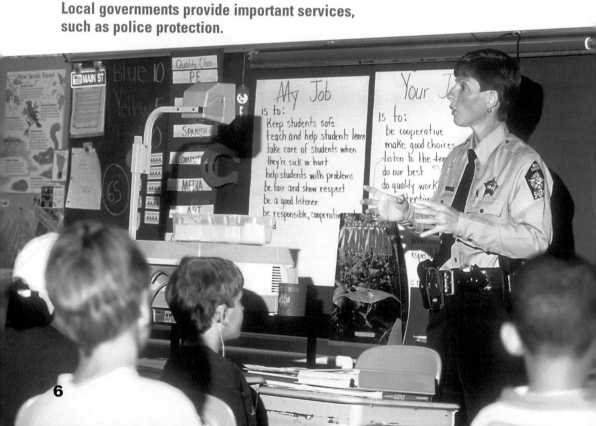

Workers from a local government keep their city's streets beautiful.

Many local governments have a **city council**. This group makes laws and decides how to spend the money raised from taxes. Some of that money keeps people safe by paying police. Some of it goes to build local parks, pick up the garbage, and run water to houses. In many cities, the voters also elect a **mayor** as the city's leader.

READING CHECK SUMMARIZE **How does local government work?**

Rules and Laws

What makes a good citizen?

As citizens, we have many rights. But we have responsibilities, too.

Good citizens obey the laws of the place where they live. Laws are rules that tell us what to do. They help keep us all safe. For example, the traffic laws tell us to drive at a safe speed and to stop at all red lights.

North Carolina's legislative branch meets in this building in Raleigh to make laws for the state.

Eva Clayton, the first woman from North Carolina elected to the United States Congress, helped make national laws.

Some laws come from the national government. Others come from the state and local governments. As citizens, we vote to decide who will serve in these governments. That way we can help make the laws we live by.

If some people do not agree with a certain law, they can work to change it. They can write to government leaders. They can ask the courts to decide if the law is fair. All of this is part of being a good citizen.

READING CHECK **GENERALIZE** What makes a good citizen?

Good Citizens

READ TO FIND OUT **How can we all be good citizens?**

What does it mean to be a good citizen? Besides obeying the laws, good citizens also vote in all elections. That way they choose the people who serve in the government and make the laws.

Some people also serve on groups that give advice to the government. For example, citizens may help choose where a new road or park should be. Good citizens also treat others fairly.

North Carolina women worked hard to win the right to vote.

Another way to be a good citizen is to help make your community a better place. Some citizens work with teachers in schools. Some help keep local parks clean. Others collect food and other goods for people who need help. When a fire or a big storm causes damage, many people work without pay to help. Even young people can play a part in making the community better.

READING CHECK SUMMARIZE **How can we all be good citizens?**

Good citizens help make their community a better place to live.

Respect for Others

READ TO FIND OUT How can people show respect for others?

One way a person can be a good citizen is to show respect for other people. For example, people follow many different religions in North Carolina. A **religion** is a person's belief system.

Some people in North Carolina are Christian. Some are Muslim, and others are Jewish. There are many religions in the world.

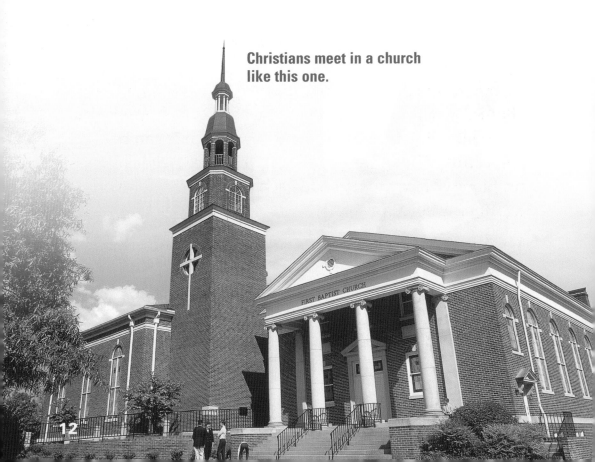

Christians meet in a church like this one.

People of different religions talked with one another as Peace Councilors.

Sometimes, people from different religions disagree about ways things should be done. But people from different religions and different backgrounds can be respectful of other people's ideas. They can talk about problems. They can listen to each other. They can work together to solve problems.

READING CHECK **SUMMARIZE** **How can people show respect for others?**

Activity 1

Identify the term that correctly matches each definition.

federal

legislative branch

executive branch

judicial branch

budget

city council

mayor

religion

1. a plan for how the government will spend money
2. the part of the government that carries out laws
3. the group that makes laws for a city
4. the government that takes care of the whole country
5. the part of the government that includes courts
6. a city leader
7. the part of the government that makes laws
8. person's belief system

Activity 2

Look at the list of words. Categorize the words in a chart like the one below. Then use a dictionary to learn the definitions of the words you do not know.

federal	toleration	bills
legislative branch	scriptures	veto
executive branch	citizen	appeal
judicial branch	public office	county seat
budget	jury	municipal
city council	political party	impeach
mayor	candidate	inauguration
religion	volunteer	

		I Know	Sounds Familiar	Don't Know
○	federal			✓
	budget		✓	
	mayor	✓		

★ **Focus Skill** **Compare and Contrast** How are the three branches of government different?

Vocabulary

1. Why might people sometimes disagree over the government's **budget**?

Recall

2. What is one of the President's duties?
3. What kinds of services do we get from the national government?
4. What are some of the ways to be a good citizen?

Critical Thinking

5. How does voting change the way we live?

Activity

Write a Letter Imagine that your local government is thinking about passing a new law. This law would not let anyone under the age of 16 ride a bicycle. Write a letter to the city council. Explain why you think this law is not fair.